A Crabtree Branches Book

IMPROVING
YOUR
SOCIAL SKILLS

WORKING AS A TEAM

VICKY BUREAU

Crabtree Publishing
crabtreebooks.com

School-to-Home Support for Caregivers and Teachers

This high-interest book is designed to motivate striving students with engaging topics while building fluency, vocabulary, and an interest in reading. Here are a few questions and activities to help the reader build upon his or her comprehension skills.

Before Reading:

- *What do I think this book is about?*
- *What do I know about this topic?*
- *What do I want to learn about this topic?*
- *Why am I reading this book?*

During Reading:

- *I wonder why...*
- *I'm curious to know...*
- *How is this like something I already know?*
- *What have I learned so far?*

After Reading:

- *What was the author trying to teach me?*
- *What are some details?*
- *How did the photographs and captions help me understand more?*
- *Read the book again and look for the vocabulary words.*
- *What questions do I still have?*

Extension Activities:

- *What was your favorite part of the book? Write a paragraph on it.*
- *Draw a picture of your favorite thing you learned from the book.*

TABLE OF CONTENTS

WHAT IS A TEAM?

Have you ever been on a team? A team is a group of people who work together.

Think back to a time when you worked with others to achieve something or **accomplish** a goal.

What were the **challenges**? What were the **successes**?

WHEN AND WHY DO WE USE TEAMS?

When do we work with others to accomplish a goal? Why is working as a team a good idea?

Maybe you work with your soccer team to win a game. You might work with your classmates to finish a group project. Maybe you work with your brother and sister to build a pillow fort. Working as a team helps you accomplish a goal or complete a task that you wouldn't be able to do on your own.

DID YOU KNOW?

Success rates improve by 88% when more than one person works toward a goal.

HOW DOES WORKING AS A TEAM HELP YOU?

When you work with others, you can accomplish more.

For example, your teammate blocks the ball from the other team and passes it to you. You kick the ball toward the other team's goal. You play soccer by working as a team.

Or your classmate writes down ideas while you draw pictures. You finish a group project by working as a team.

HOW DOES WORKING AS A TEAM HELP OTHERS?

You can help others accomplish their goals through **cooperation** and working as a team.

Cooperation means you work with others. It also means that you set **roles**, understand **responsibilities**, and **appreciate** the work of others. When you cooperate, you work together to get something done.

TEAMWORK AND THE BRAIN

Teamwork can also be good for your brain. Bonding with others releases a chemical called **oxytocin**. This chemical is released by your brain and can make you feel appreciated, accomplished, and **fulfilled**.

CHECKPOINT:
RELATING TO THE
REAL WORLD

Can you remember a time when you cooperated with others to achieve something? How did it make you feel? Did you share this feeling of success with your team?

Can you remember a time when you cooperated with others and you did not achieve something? How did it make you feel? Did you share this feeling of defeat with your team?

HOW WE WORK WITH OTHERS

How do you work with others?

How can you get better at working with others?

In order to effectively work as a team, you need to create roles. A role is a team member's job, or task, in accomplishing a goal.

Effective cooperation also includes responsibilities. A responsibility is something that each role is expected to do.

DID YOU KNOW?

The ideal team is five to nine people.

WHY WE WORK WITH OTHERS

We cooperate, or work with others, because it helps us achieve something we can't do on our own.

Think about the cookie jar you can't reach. You may work as team with your big sister to get to your favorite chocolate chip cookies.

When you don't understand the new math lesson, you may work with others as a study group to help each other understand how to solve equations.

Sometimes we can't successfully do something on our own. Sometimes, we need to work together to find success.

UNDERSTANDING EVERYONE'S ROLE

An important part about working as a team is to create, understand, and appreciate every person's role in the group. When everyone knows their role on a team and does it to the best of their ability, it creates a stronger, more successful team.

In sports, team roles are called positions.

In school, student roles are called duties.

In society, people's roles are called jobs.

CHALLENGES TO WORKING AS A TEAM

Working as part of a team can pose **challenges** at times.

You may not like or agree with the way someone is doing something.

It's important to understand and appreciate that roles are different because people are different. Everyone has different strengths and weaknesses.

A soccer goalie may be better than you at blocking.

A classmate may be better than you at drawing.

It's important to understand that when you cooperate, you and your team share the success.

DID YOU KNOW?

Working as part of a team can help boost your self-esteem.

BENEFITS OF WORKING AS A TEAM

Working as a team can be very fulfilling. Achieving a goal together can make you feel accomplished, **proud**, and successful.

By believing in your team, you learn to believe in yourself!

DID YOU KNOW?

Some of the most effective teams don't have leaders.

DO TEAMS NEED LEADERS?

Not every team needs a leader. By effectively creating roles, understanding responsibilities, and appreciating the work of others, teams can successfully complete a task without the need for a leader. In other words, the task is shared, and everyone cooperates to accomplish the goal.

CHECKPOINT:
RELATING TO THE REAL WORLD

Think about a time you were part of a team.

What was your role on the team?

What were your responsibilities?

How did you make sure you could fulfill your responsibilities on your team?

GLOSSARY

accomplish (uh·KOM·plish): Complete successfully

appreciate (uh·PREE·shee·eyt): To understand the importance of something

challenge (CHA·luhnj): A difficult problem

cooperation (koh·op·uh·RAY·shun): Working together to get something done

fulfilled (ful·FILD): Feeling satisfied and happy

oxytocin (ok·see·TOH·suhn) A hormone that acts on organs in the body, including the brain

proud (PROWD): Feeling very happy and pleased about something you have done

responsibilities (ruh·spaan·suh·BIL·uh·teez): Things you are expected to do

role (ROHL): The job someone has in a particular activity or situation

success (suhk·SES): The achievement of something you have been trying to do

INDEX

WEBSITES TO VISIT

pbs.org/parents/crafts-and-experiments/simple-teamwork-games

bookwidgets.com/blog/2019/10/15-fun-team-building-activities-and-
   trust-games-for-the-classroom

youtube.com/c/RocketKids/search?query=teamwork

ABOUT THE AUTHOR

Vicky Bureau was born in Longueuil, Quebec, and was raised in South Florida. As a teacher, she developed a passion for the social and emotional growth of her students and later transitioned into the area of child and adolescent psychology after earning her master's degree in school counseling. In addition to working with children, Vicky loves to be surrounded by animals and nature. She lives in Fort Lauderdale with her family: Billy, Khloe, M.J., and Max; her three cats, Alley, Baguette, and Salem; and her dog, Boomer.

Written by: Vicky Bureau
Designed by: Rhea Magaro Wallace
Interior designed by: Kathy Walsh
Series Development: James Earley
Proofreader: Melissa Boyce
Educational Consultant: Marie Lemke M.Ed.

Photographs: Shutterstock Cover robert_s, Viktoriia Protsak, DGLimages; Background robert_s; Color Splash Viktoriia Protsak, Box p 7, 17, 23, 26 Puwadol Jaturawutthichai; p 5 Monkey Business Images; p 7 SpeedKingz; p 9 muzsy; p 11 Daisy Daisy; p 12 SewCream; p 13 Ground Picture; p 14 matimix; p 15 katatonia82; p 17 Ground Picture; p 19 stockfour; p 21 dotshock; p 23 Monkey Business Images; p 24 Monkey Business Images; p 26 Monkey Business Images; p 29 Lopolo

Crabtree Publishing

crabtreebooks.com 800-387-7650

Copyright © 2023 Crabtree Publishing

Printed in the U.S.A./012023/CG20220815

Published in Canada
Crabtree Publishing
616 Welland Ave.
St. Catharines, Ontario
L2M 5V6

Published in the United States
Crabtree Publishing
347 Fifth Ave
Suite 1402-145
New York, NY 10016

Library and Archives Canada Cataloguing in Publication
Available at Library and Archives Canada

Library of Congress Cataloging-in-Publication Data
Available at the Library of Congress

Hardcover: 978-1-0396-6048-9
Paperback: 978-1-0396-6243-8
Ebook (pdf): 978-1-0396-7039-6
Epub: 978-1-0396-7237-6